MATTER OF FACTS

A collection of 365 fun facts

BY

JAY MIRCHANDANEY

Chennai • Bangalore

CLEVER FOX PUBLISHING
Chennai, India

Published by CLEVER FOX PUBLISHING 2025
Copyright © Jay Mirchandaney 2025

All Rights Reserved.
ISBN: 978-93-67070-67-3

This book has been published with all reasonable efforts taken to make the material error-free after the consent of the author. No part of this book shall be used, reproduced in any manner whatsoever without written permission from the author, except in the case of brief quotations embodied in critical articles and reviews.

The Author of this book is solely responsible and liable for its content including but not limited to the views, representations, descriptions, statements, information, opinions and references ["Content"]. The Content of this book shall not constitute or be construed or deemed to reflect the opinion or expression of the Publisher or Editor. Neither the Publisher nor Editor endorse or approve the Content of this book or guarantee the reliability, accuracy or completeness of the Content published herein and do not make any representations or warranties of any kind, express or implied, including but not limited to the implied warranties of merchantability, fitness for a particular purpose. The Publisher and Editor shall not be liable whatsoever for any errors, omissions, whether such errors or omissions result from negligence, accident, or any other cause or claims for loss or damages of any kind, including without limitation, indirect or consequential loss or damage arising out of use, inability to use, or about the reliability, accuracy or sufficiency of the information contained in this book.

CONTENTS

Disclaimer xi
Foreword xiii

1. The Origin of the Word "Fact" 1
2. The World's First Skyscraper 1
3. Snakes and Ladders 2
4. Barcode Scanners 2
5. Chess 3
6. Toast 3
7. Prime Numbers 4
8. The Theft Of The Mona Lisa 4
9. FIFA World Cup 5
10. Marvel Comics 5
11. Nike 6
12. Mozart 6
13. Thriller 7
14. The Barcode 7
15. Youtube 8
16. Checkers 8
17. Rubik's Cube 9
18. First Ever Skate Park 9
19. Burj Khalifa Elevator 10
20. USB 10
21. Periodic Table 11
22. Armadillo 11
23. Heartless 12
24. Jellyfish 12
25. Bees 13
26. Water 13
27. Dog 14
28. Shopping 14
29. Kangaroo 15
30. Television 15
31. "E" 16
32. Santa Claus 16
33. Yawn 17
34. Video Games 17
35. France 18
36. Fingers 18
37. Doritos 19
38. Lightning 19

39. Hippopotomonstrosesquippedaliophobia 20
40. Cats 20
41. Aglet 21
42. M & M 21
43. National Anthem 22
44. Great Wall of China 22
45. Chewing Gum 23
46. Nostrils 23
47. Moonquakes 24
48. Earth 24
49. Mars 25
50. Laser 25
51. Belize Flag 26
52. NBA 26
53. Super Bowl 27
54. Charlie Chaplin 27
55. Ukulele 28
56. Cyber Attacks 28
57. London in USA 29
58. Oxygen 29
59. Marvel Comic 30
60. Starbucks 30
61. Walk on the Moon 31
62. Blink 31
63. Heartbeat 32
64. Lion's Vision 32
65. Queen Elizabeth II 33
66. 1st Cricket World Cup 33
67. Tennis Match 34
68. Augustus Caesar 34
69. Khmer 35
70. Julius Caesar 35
71. Papua New Guinea 36
72. Oldest Operational Airline 36
73. Longest Natural Arch 37
74. Mona Lisa – 16 Years 37
75. Fastest Mile 38
76. Driver-Less Rail System 38
77. Busiest Pedestrian Crossing 39
78. Rugby 39
79. Lego 40
80. 1st Cricket World Cup Winner 40
81. Bitcoin 41
82. Piano 41
83. U2 42
84. Pit Stop 42
85. British Pound 43
86. Longest Roller Coaster 43

Contents

87. Heaviest Building 44
88. Pizza Delivery in Space 44
89. Human Skull 45
90. New Year 45
91. No "A" 46
92. Bowling 46
93. Halloween 47
94. Overdue Book 47
95. Amazon 48
96. Shortest National Anthem 48
97. Indian Flag 49
98. Wimbledon 49
99. Largest Sun Dial 50
100. Elephant's Trunk 50
101. Landlocked by Landlocked 51
102. Sticky Rice 51
103. 4th of July 52
104. Birthday Buddy 52
105. Tea 53
106. Lionel Messi 53
107. Banana 54
108. Nobel Prize 54
109. Hollywood Walk of Fame 55
110. Suriname 55
111. Italy 56
112. Quarantine 56
113. Arnold Schwarzenegger 57
114. Saudi Arabia 57
115. Test Match 58
116. Coldest Inhabited Place 58
117. Hottest Inhabited Place 59
118. Mumbai 59
119. Prince 60
120. Tajikistan 60
121. Berlin 61
122. Colour Photograph 61
123. 18 Muscles 62
124. Australia 62
125. Kangaroos 63
126. BMW 63
127. Saxophone 64
128. Nobel Peace Prize 64
129. Bubble Wrap 65
130. Tree Planting Record 65
131. Kazakhstan 66
132. Tetris 66
133. Jaguar 67

Contents

134. Brain 67
135. Caesar Salad 68
136. French 68
137. World War II Casualties 69
138. Digital Currency 69
139. Carbon Negative 70
140. Leap Day 70
141. Fraction 71
142. Barack Obama 71
143. China 72
144. Metallica 72
145. Jamaica 73
146. January 73
147. C - Language 74
148. Napoleon Bonaparte 74
149. Rain-Drop 75
150. Moon's Diameter 75
151. Earth's Diameter 76
152. Potato in Space 76
153. Beatles 77
154. Earth's Orbital Speed 77
155. Dolphins 78
156. Plane Crash 78
157. Monarch 79
158. UNO 79
159. Island Nation 80
160. Pyramids 80
161. Philippines 81
162. Waddle 81
163. A for Australia 82
164. Cuba 82
165. Ice 83
166. Harp 83
167. RGB 84
168. Violin 84
169. Overmorrow 85
170. Smallest Guitar 85
171. Alphabet 86
172. The Himalayas 86
173. Yahoo 87
174. Pin 87
175. Avatar 88
176. Snickers 88
177. Nauru 89
178. Metric System 89
179. Biggest Guitar 90
180. Big Ben 90
181. Vincent Van Gogh 91
182. Dubai Mall 91
183. Pears 92
184. Basketball 92
185. One Eye Open 93
186. Greece 93

Contents

187. Plastic Bottle 94
188. Car 94
189. First Computer 95
190. Pomology 95
191. Talc 96
192. Barrel 96
193. Lego Production 97
194. Skulk 97
195. Dannebrog 98
196. Chromophobia 98
197. Forests 99
198. -200 Deg Celsius 99
199. Helicopter 100
200. Most Visited Country 100
201. Garage Start Ups 101
202. Earths Circumference 101
203. Blackletter 102
204. Dash 102
205. Horses 103
206. Band-Aid 103
207. Walt Disney 104
208. Speed of Light 104
209. Parker 51 105
210. Nokia 1100 105
211. Fire 106
212. Grocery Shopping 106
213. Mouse 107
214. Melting Point 107
215. Corn 108
216. Adidas & Puma 108
217. Checkmate 109
218. Seconds in a Week 109
219. The Statue of Liberty 110
220. Accident 110
221. August 111
222. B for Billion 111
223. Sun 112
224. Weight on Mars 112
225. Alphabet "J" 113
226. Abstemious 113
227. Antarctica 114
228. Porsche 114
229. Jam or Marmalade 115
230. 111111111 115
231. Math 116
232. Tomatoes 116
233. Headphones 117
234. Jiffy 117
235. Melting Point of Gold 118
236. Dogs 118

237.	First Web Page 119	264.	Air Conditioners 132
238.	Train 119	265.	Gravity 133
239.	3 Dogs 120	266.	Cuckoo Clock 133
240.	Strawberries 120	267.	Cornflakes 134
241.	80 kmph 121	268.	Email 134
242.	Cotton Candy 121	269.	Smallest Bone 135
243.	Coalition 122	270.	The Moon 135
244.	Dreamt 122	271.	2 Stomachs 136
245.	Mars – God of War 123	272.	The Doorbell 136
246.	Jupiter 123	273.	Mona Lisa 137
247.	Potato 124	274.	Google 137
248.	Flute 124	275.	Bale 138
249.	Microwave 125	276.	Elephants 138
250.	Square Flag 125	277.	1 Year 139
251.	Disney World 126	278.	Moonlight 139
252.	Volcanoes 126	279.	Orange 140
253.	Zero 127	280.	Not Berries 140
254.	Four 127	281.	Berries 141
255.	Forty 128	282.	Parliament 141
256.	Seven 128	283.	1700 Words 142
257.	Lemniscate 129	284.	Pringles Chip 142
258.	Rhythm 129	285.	Captcha 143
259.	Folding Chair 130	286.	The Jazz Singer 143
260.	Sprinkler 130	287.	Shiver 144
261.	Birds 131	288.	Flamboyance 144
262.	Windmill 131	289.	Nordic Cross 145
263.	Tower 132	290.	Left-Handed 145

291. Taste Buds 146
292. Diamond Rain 146
293. Lethologica 147
294. Aibohphobia 147
295. Baby Flamingos 148
296. Turn Orange 148
297. Muscles 149
298. lol 149
299. Army 150
300. 3 Hearts 150
301. #Love 151
302. First Television Advertisement 151
303. The Last Supper 152
304. Netherlands 152
305. Abu Dhabi 153
306. Taylor Swift 153
307. Honey 154
308. Ballpoint Pen 154
309. Fingerprints 155
310. Cloud 155
311. Daylight Saving 156
312. Nepal 156
313. Earth's Rotation 157
314. Sheep v/s Human 157
315. Brain Burns Calories 158
316. Skin 158
317. Northern Hemisphere 159
318. Australia- Wider than the Moon 159
319. Eiffel Tower 160
320. Pyramids - Sudan 160
321. Finland 161
322. Heartbeats 161
323. Russia 162
324. Tug of War 162
325. Longest Car 163
326. Centre of the Earth 163
327. Largest Castle 164
328. Guinness Book 164
329. Montreal Tower 165
330. USA's capital 165
331. Teeth 166
332. Shortest War 166
333. Sea World – Abu Dhabi 167
334. Ostrich's Eye 167
335. Sneeze 168
336. Hashtag 168
337. Africa 169
338. Tongue Print 169
339. Hollywood 170

340. Eiffel Tower During the Summer 170
341. Hum 171
342. Speeding Ticket 171
343. Venus 172
344. Heart 172
345. Lungs 173
346. Diamonds 173
347. Pineapple 174
348. Kitkat 174
349. Pigs 175
350. Nails 175
351. Ketchup 176
352. Bamboo 176
353. Hippopotamus 177
354. Cows Have Accents 177
355. Carrots 178
356. Spaghetto 178
357. Pencil 179
358. Lewis Hamilton 179
359. Novak Djokovic 180
360. Spencer Gore 180
361. Chess Grandmaster 181
362. Oldest NBA Team 181
363. Largest Hotel 182
364. Bill Russell 182
365. Goodbye 183

DISCLAIMER

The fun facts presented in this book were collected from various internet sources by an enthusiastic researcher between the age of 10 to 13.

While every effort has been made to ensure the accuracy of these facts at the time of writing, some information may have been updated or changed since then.

Please consider this book as a light-hearted compilation rather than a definitive reference.

FOREWORD

As a ten-year-old during the beginning of the COVID-19 lockdowns with a love for learning and too much free time, I started a blog called "Fact of the Day." As the title says, I would post one fun fact every day and would cross-check its accuracy with three different sources.

It took me 1,250 days (and therefore 1,250 facts) to finally decide that I was done with the blog. So, that would mean that on the website I created with much help from my parents, mirchandaney.com/fact, I had a boatload of information that lots of people may find interesting.

I realized that my website, which I made no effort to market to other people, probably wasn't very accessible and that if I moved this information into other formats then anyone who wanted to learn something new could benefit.

After some contemplation, the format I decided upon was a book. The main objective of this book is to share fun information on my blog, so all proceeds from this book will be going towards various charitable causes.

I hope you enjoy reading and exploring these tidbits of knowledge!

-Jay

1. THE ORIGIN OF THE WORD "FACT"

The word fact is derived from the Latin word *facere* which means "*do.*"

2. THE WORLD'S FIRST SKYSCRAPER

Chicago's Home Insurance Building, which was built in 1885 and was 42.1 metres tall, is considered to be the world's first skyscraper.

3. SNAKES AND LADDERS

The board game 'Snakes and Ladders' was invented in India during the second century CE!

4. BARCODE SCANNERS

Barcode scanners scan the white spaces, not the black ones!

5. CHESS

There are more possible iterations of a game of chess than there are atoms in the known universe!

6. TOAST

The chemical reaction that turns bread into toast is called the Maillard Reaction.

7. PRIME NUMBERS

2 and 3 are the only consecutive prime numbers.

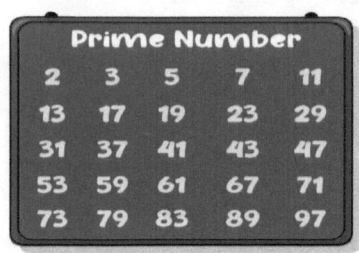

8. THE THEFT OF THE MONA LISA

Pablo Picasso was one of the suspects in the theft of the Mona Lisa!

9. FIFA WORLD CUP

Uruguay hosted and won the first-ever FIFA World Cup!

10. MARVEL COMICS

Marvel's first comic was published in October of 1939!

11. NIKE

Between the years 1964 and 1971, Nike was known as Blue Ribbon Sports!

12. MOZART

Mozart composed his first piece of published music at just five years old!

13. THRILLER

Michael Jackson's Thriller sold approximately 70 million copies worldwide, making it the best-selling album of all time!

14. THE BARCODE

The barcode was invented in 1948 by an American inventor named Norman Joseph Woodland.

15. YOUTUBE

Approximately 720,000 hours of video is uploaded to YouTube everyday!

16. CHECKERS

The game of checkers has roughly 5×10^{20} possible positions!

17. RUBIK'S CUBE

A Rubik's cube has more than 43 quintillion different permutations!

18. FIRST EVER SKATE PARK

The world's first skate park (named Surf City) was built in 1965.

19. BURJ KHALIFA ELEVATOR

The Burj Khalifa's elevator moves at a speed of 10 metres per second!

20. USB

USB stands for Universal Serial Bus!

21. PERIODIC TABLE

The only letter on the periodic table that doesn't appear is J.

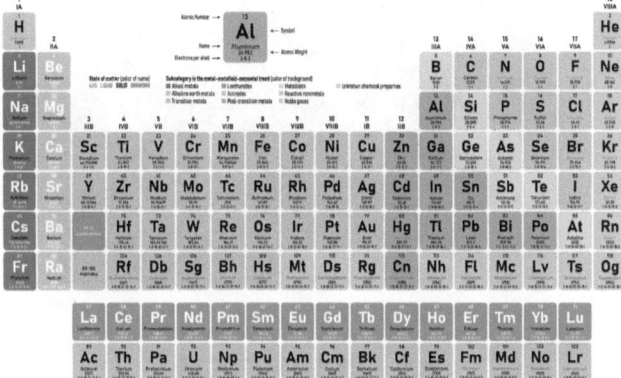

22. ARMADILLO

An armadillo's shell is so hard it can deflect a bullet!

Matter of Facts

23. HEARTLESS

Jellyfish don't have hearts!

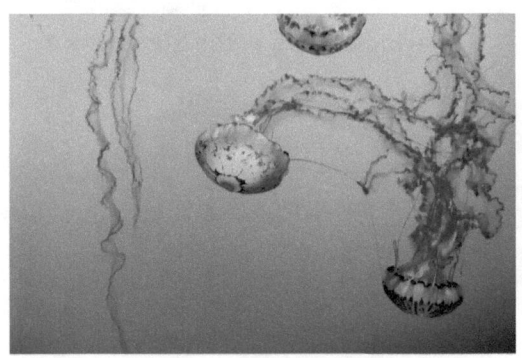

24. JELLYFISH

Jellyfish are 95% water!

25. BEES

Bees can fly higher than Mount Everest!

26. WATER

Water makes different pouring sounds depending on its temperature!

27. DOG

A dog's nose is like our fingerprints; it is unique to each dog.

28. SHOPPING

An average male gets bored on a shopping trip after 26 minutes!

29. KANGAROO

If you lift a kangaroo's tail, it can't hop!

30. TELEVISION

The TV was invented only 2 years after the invention of sliced bread!

Matter of Facts   15

31. "E"

Every odd number has an "E" in it!

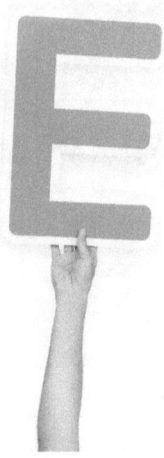

32. SANTA CLAUS

Santa Claus has a red suit because of Coca-Cola's advertising campaigns.

33. YAWN

The bigger your brain, the longer you yawn!

34. VIDEO GAMES

Doctors who play video games for more than 3 hours a week make fewer operating room errors.

35. FRANCE

France is the largest country in the European Union.

36. FINGERS

There are no muscles in your fingers!

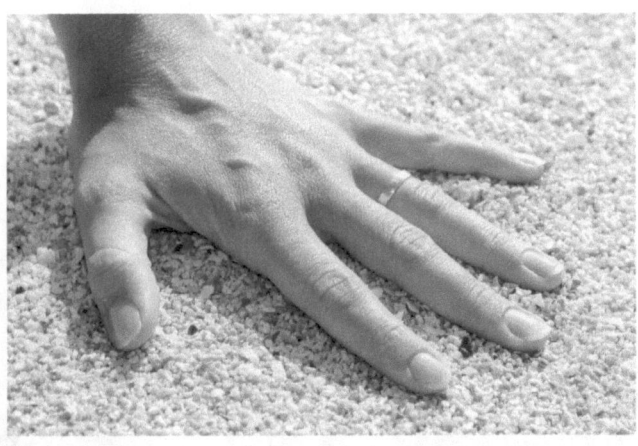

37. DORITOS

A bag of Doritos is 48% air!

38. LIGHTNING

A bolt of lightning is five times hotter than the sun!

39. HIPPOPOTOMONSTROSESQUIPPEDALIOPHOBIA

Hippopotomonstrosesquippedaliophobia is one of the longest words in the dictionary. Ironically, it's the term used for the phobia of long words.

40. CATS

Cats can't taste sweet things!

41. AGLET

The plastic tip of a shoelace is called an *aglet*.

42. M & M

M & M stands for Mars and Murrie.

43. NATIONAL ANTHEM

The Spanish national anthem has no words.

44. GREAT WALL OF CHINA

The Great Wall of China is 21,196 km long. That's 1,927 football fields!

45. CHEWING GUM

Chewing gum increases concentration.

46. NOSTRILS

Your nostrils work one at a time!

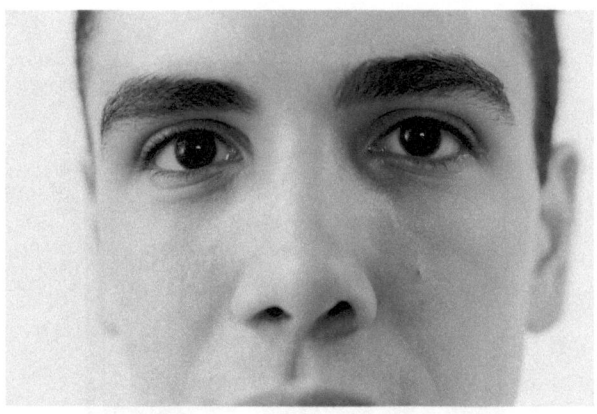

47. MOONQUAKES

The Moon has "moonquakes!"

48. EARTH

The only planet in our solar system that isn't named after a god is Earth!

49. MARS

687 days is one year on Mars.

50. LASER

The word "laser" is an acronym, it stands for Light Amplification of Stimulated Emission of Radiation.

51. BELIZE FLAG

The flag of Belize consists of 12 different colours, making it the most colourful flag in the world.

52. NBA

The first ever NBA game was played on the 1st of November, 1946 in Toronto, Canada.

53. SUPER BOWL

The first-ever Super Bowl happened on the 15th of January, 1967.

54. CHARLIE CHAPLIN

On the 6th of July 1925, Charlie Chaplin became the first actor to appear on the cover of Time Magazine.

55. UKULELE

The ukulele was invented in the year 1879.

56. CYBER ATTACKS

On an average day, more than 220 cyber attacks occur.

57. LONDON IN USA

There are three cities in the USA named London.

London, Ohio   London, Kentucky   London, Arkansas

58. OXYGEN

On average, a tree produces 117 kilograms of oxygen per year.

59. MARVEL COMIC

Marvel's first comic was published in October of 1939.

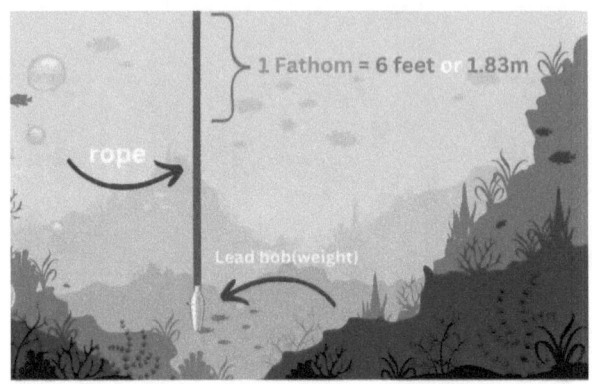

60. STARBUCKS

The world's largest Starbucks is in Chicago and occupies over 10,000 square meters of space.

61. WALK ON THE MOON

Only 12 people have walked on the Moon.

62. BLINK

On average, the human eye blinks more than 15,000 times per day.

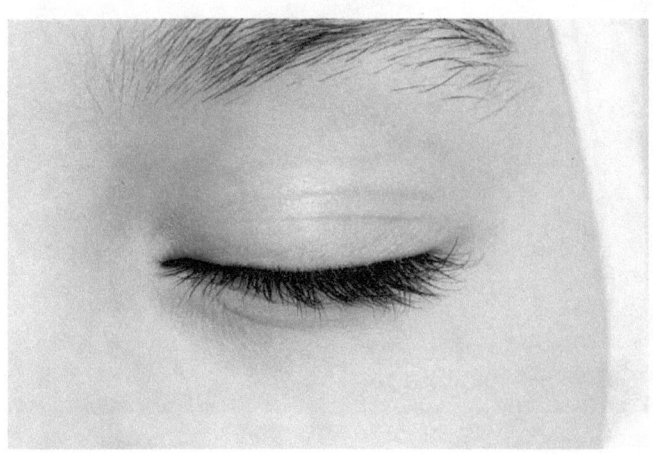

63. HEARTBEAT

You can hear a blue whale's heartbeat from three kilometers away.

64. LION'S VISION

A lion's vision is around eight times better than that of a human.

65. QUEEN ELIZABETH II

Queen Elizabeth II was crowned on the 2nd of June 1953.

66. 1ST CRICKET WORLD CUP

The first Cricket World Cup was held in 1975.

67. TENNIS MATCH

The world's longest tennis match lasted for 11 hours and 5 minutes.

68. AUGUSTUS CAESAR

The month of August was named after Roman emperor Augustus Caesar.

69. KHMER

Khmer (the official language of Cambodia) has 74 letters in its alphabet, more than any other language.

ក គ ខ ឃ ង៉ ង
ka ko kha kho nga ngo

ច ជ ឆ ឈ ញ៉ ញ
ca co cha cho ña ño

ដ ឌ ត ទ ថ ធ ប៉ ណ ន
da do ta to tha tho tha tho na no

ប បិ ប៉ ព ផ ភ ម៉ ម
ba bo pa po pha pho ma mo

យ៉ យ រ៉ រ ឡ ល វ៉ វ
ya yo ra ro la lo wa wo

ស ស៊ ហ ហ៊ី អ អ៊
sa so ha ho qa qo

ហ្គ ហ្គ៊ ហ្វ ហ្វ៊ ហ្ស ហ្ស៊
ga go fa fo ža žo

70. JULIUS CAESAR

The month of July was named after Roman dictator Julius Caesar.

71. PAPUA NEW GUINEA

Papua New Guinea has more spoken languages than any other country– 840 languages!

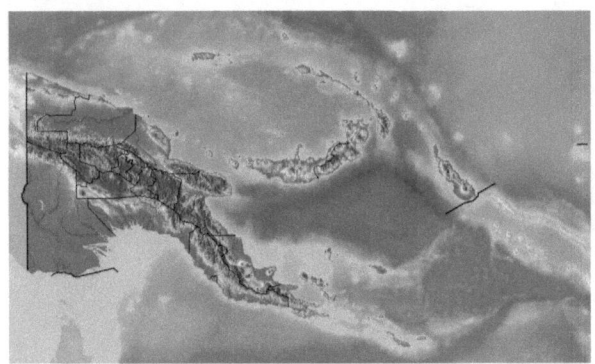

72. OLDEST OPERATIONAL AIRLINE

A Dutch airline named KLM has been in operation since 1919, making it the oldest currently operational airline in the world.

73. LONGEST NATURAL ARCH

China's Xianren spans approximately 121.9 metres, making it the longest natural arch in the world.

74. MONA LISA – 16 YEARS

The Mona Lisa took approximately sixteen years for Leonardo Da Vinci to paint.

75. FASTEST MILE

In 1999, Hicham El Guerrouj ran the world's fastest mile, with a time of 3 minutes 43.13 seconds.

76. DRIVER-LESS RAIL SYSTEM

The Dubai Metro is the world's longest driver-less rail system at 74.6 kilometres long.

77. BUSIEST PEDESTRIAN CROSSING

Japan's Shibuya Crossing is the busiest pedestrian crossing in the world, with as many as 3,000 people crossing at a time.

78. RUGBY

Rugby was invented in England in the year 1823.

79. LEGO

The Lego Group was founded on the 10th of August, 1932, by a Danish carpenter named Ole Kirk Christiansen.

80. 1ST CRICKET WORLD CUP WINNER

The West Indies won the first-ever ICC Cricket World Cup.

81. BITCOIN

Bitcoin was created in 2008 by an unidentified individual going by the pseudonym Satoshi Nakamoto.

82. PIANO

The piano was invented in the year 1700 by an Italian man named Bartolomeo Cristofori.

83. U2

Irish rock band U2 has won more Grammy Awards than any other group: 22.

84. PIT STOP

The average Formula One pit stop is 3 seconds long.

85. BRITISH POUND

The British pound is more than 1,200 years old, making it the world's oldest currency still in use.

86. LONGEST ROLLER COASTER

The Steel Dragon 2000 roller coaster in Japan is 2,479 metres long, making it the longest roller coaster in the world!

87. HEAVIEST BUILDING

The Palace of the Parliament in Romania weighs approximately 4.1 million tonnes, making it the heaviest building in the world.

88. PIZZA DELIVERY IN SPACE

In 2001, Pizza Hut spent $1 million to deliver a pizza to the International Space Station.

89. HUMAN SKULL

An average human skull weighs approximately five kilograms.

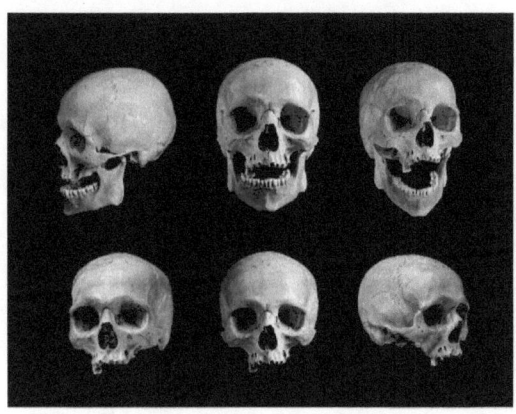

90. NEW YEAR

Kiribati is the first country to welcome the new year each year!

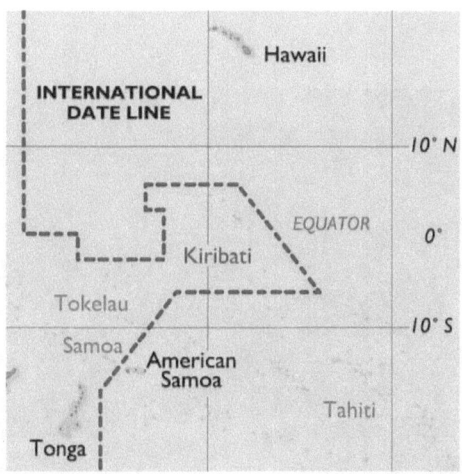

91. NO "A"

No number written in word form before one thousand contains the letter 'a'.

Number Words

0	zero	10	ten	20	twenty
1	one	11	eleven	30	thirty
2	two	12	twelve	40	forty
3	three	13	thirteen	50	fifty
4	four	14	fourteen	60	sixty
5	five	15	fifteen	70	seventy
6	six	16	sixteen	80	eighty
7	seven	17	seventeen	90	ninety
8	eight	18	eighteen	100	one hundred
9	nine	19	nineteen	1,000	one thousand

92. BOWLING

The world's first indoor bowling alley opened on the 1st of January, 1840.

93. HALLOWEEN

Halloween originated in Ireland!

94. OVERDUE BOOK

The most overdue library book was 288 years late.

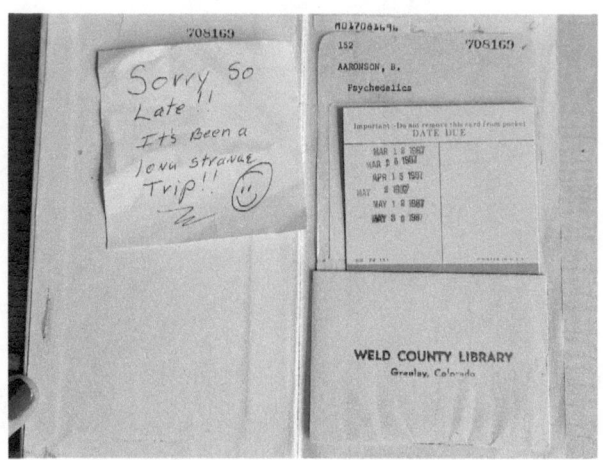

95. AMAZON

Amazon was originally named "Cadabra."

96. SHORTEST NATIONAL ANTHEM

The national anthem of Japan has just 4 lines, making it the shortest national anthem in the world.

97. INDIAN FLAG

India's national flag was created by an Indian freedom fighter named Pingali Venakayya.

98. WIMBLEDON

Wimbledon started in 1877, making it the oldest tennis tournament in the world!

99. LARGEST SUN DIAL

India's Samrat Yantra (translated to 'Supreme Instrument') is the largest sundial in the world.

100. ELEPHANT'S TRUNK

An elephant can hold upto 11 litres of water in it's trunk!

101. LANDLOCKED BY LANDLOCKED

Liechtenstein and Uzbekistan are the only two countries in the world which are landlocked by other landlocked countries.

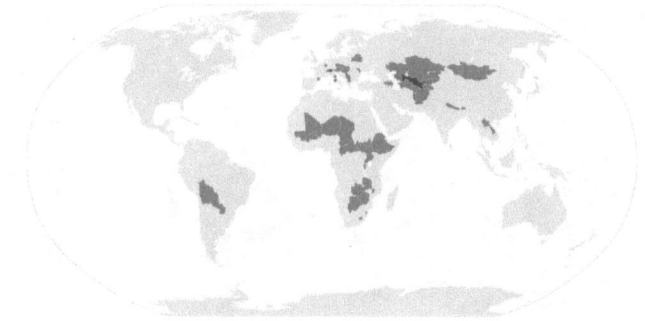

102. STICKY RICE

The Great Wall of China is held together by sticky rice.

103. 4TH OF JULY

Three U.S. Presidents died on the 4th of July!

104. BIRTHDAY BUDDY

Charles Darwin and Abraham Lincoln were born on the same day.

105. TEA

Tea is the second-most consumed beverage in the world after water.

106. LIONEL MESSI

Lionel Messi has played in 26 FIFA World Cup matches, more than any other football player.

107. BANANA

Bananas are the most cultivated fruits in the world.

108. NOBEL PRIZE

Marie Curie is only person to earn Nobel prizes in two different science categories.

109. HOLLYWOOD WALK OF FAME

Frank Sinatra has three stars on the Hollywood Walk of Fame; one for music, one for movies, and one for television.

110. SURINAME

Approximately 94.6% of Suriname's surface area is forest.

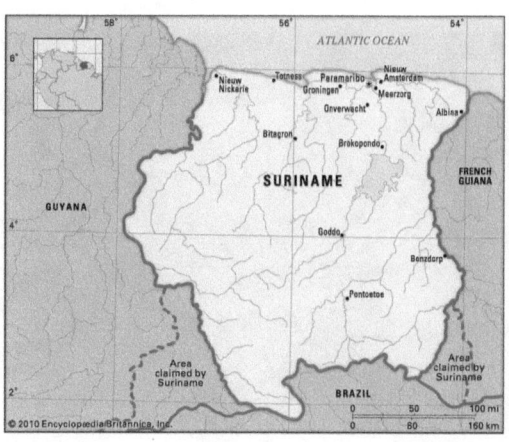

Matter of Facts

111. ITALY

Italy has the highest amount of UNESCO World Heritage Sites in the world.

112. QUARANTINE

The word 'quarantine' comes from the Italian word *quarantina* which means forty days.

113. ARNOLD SCHWARZENEGGER

Arnold Schwarzenegger received $21,429 for each word he said in the movie Terminator II.

114. SAUDI ARABIA

Saudi Arabia is the largest country in the world that has no rivers.

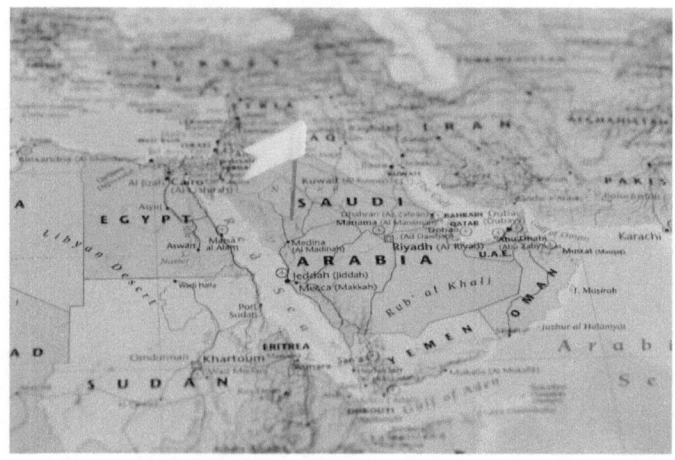

115. TEST MATCH

The longest cricket test match lasted nine days.

116. COLDEST INHABITED PLACE

The coldest inhabited place in the world is Oymyakon, Russia.

117. HOTTEST INHABITED PLACE

The hottest inhabited place in the world is Dallol, Ethiopia.

118. MUMBAI

Mumbai has a coastline of about 150 kilometres.

119. PRINCE

Prince played 27 instruments on his debut album.

120. TAJIKISTAN

Over 90% of Tajikistan's territory is mountainous.

121. BERLIN

Berlin is 9 times bigger than Paris.

122. COLOUR PHOTOGRAPH

The first colour photograph was taken in 1861.

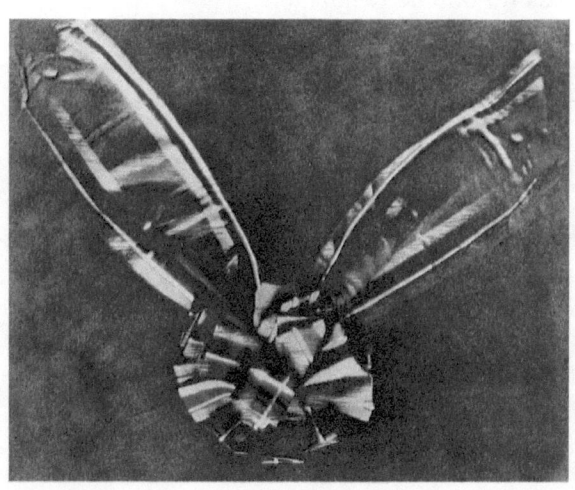

123. 18 MUSCLES

Dogs have 18 muscles in each of their ears.

124. AUSTRALIA

Australia has no official language.

125. KANGAROOS

Australia has more kangaroos than people.

126. BMW

BMW stands for Bayerische Motoren Werke.

127. SAXOPHONE

Saxophones were invented by a Belgian inventor Adolphe Sax.

128. NOBEL PEACE PRIZE

Theodore Roosevelt was the first US President to win a Nobel Peace Prize.

129. BUBBLE WRAP

Bubble wrap was originally invented as wallpaper.

130. TREE PLANTING RECORD

In 2015, a team of 100 volunteers in Bhutan set a world record by planting 49,762 trees in an hour.

131. KAZAKHSTAN

Kazakhstan is the world's largest landlocked country.

132. TETRIS

Tetris was the first video-game played in space.

133. JAGUAR

The word 'jaguar' comes from the Native American word *yaguar*, which means 'he who kills with one leap'

134. BRAIN

The human brain is ~75% water.

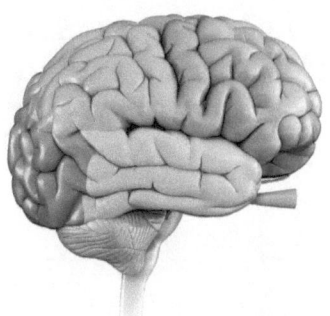

135. CAESAR SALAD

Caesar salads were invented in Mexico.

136. FRENCH

French was the official language of England from 1066 to 1362.

137. WORLD WAR II CASUALTIES

~3% of the world's population in 1939 died in World War II.

138. DIGITAL CURRENCY

Approximately 92% of the world's currency is digital, most of the money you earn, transact with, use to buy goods and services, and so on exists only on computers and hard drives.

139. CARBON NEGATIVE

Bhutan is the only carbon-negative country in the world.

140. LEAP DAY

The odds of being born on February 29th are about 1 in 1,461.

141. FRACTION

The word fraction is derived from the Latin word "fractio" which means "breaking"

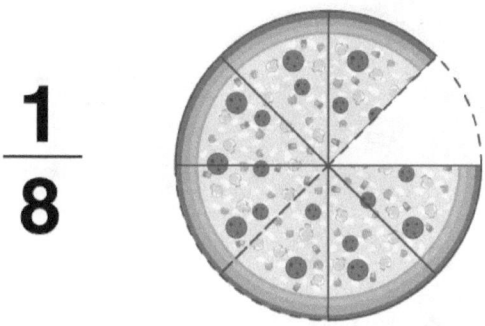

142. BARACK OBAMA

Barack Obama has won two Grammy awards.

143. CHINA

China borders 14 countries.

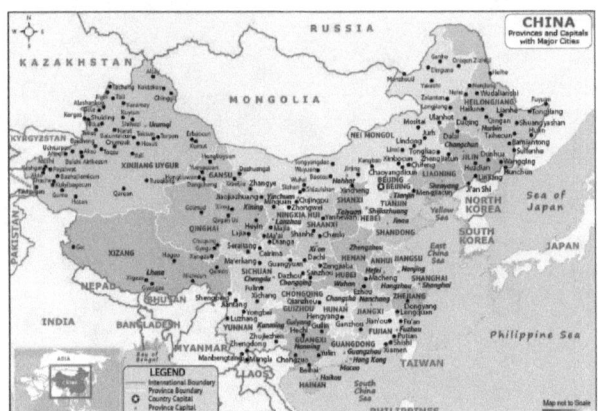

144. METALLICA

Metallica is the only band that has played on all seven continents.

145. JAMAICA

The only country without red, white, or blue in their flag is Jamaica.

146. JANUARY

January is named after the Roman god of beginnings and endings, Janus!

147. C - LANGUAGE

The programming language C was invented by an American computer scientist named Dennis Ritchie.

148. NAPOLEON BONAPARTE

The French military leader Napoleon Bonaparte wrote a romance novel *Clisson et Eugénie*.

149. RAIN-DROP

On average, a raindrop takes two minutes to reach the ground.

150. MOON'S DIAMETER

The Moon's diameter is 3,474.8 kilometers.

151. EARTH'S DIAMETER

The Earth's diameter is 12,742 kilometers.

152. POTATO IN SPACE

In October 1995, the potato became the first vegetable to be grown in space.

153. BEATLES

The Beatles have officially released 227 songs.

154. EARTH'S ORBITAL SPEED

The average orbital speed of Earth is about 30 kilometers per second.

155. DOLPHINS

Dolphins are capable of hearing sounds underwater from as far as 24 kilometres away.

156. PLANE CRASH

On average, your chance of dying in a plane crash is one in eleven million.

157. MONARCH

Currently, there are 43 countries in the world with a monarch as the head of state.

158. UNO

Uno was invented in 1971.

159. ISLAND NATION

Indonesia is the world's largest island nation.

160. PYRAMIDS

The Pyramids of Giza took 20 years build.

161. PHILIPPINES

The Philippines consists of 7,641 islands.

162. WADDLE

A group of penguins is called a waddle.

163. A FOR AUSTRALIA

The word "Australia" has three A's that are all pronounced differently.

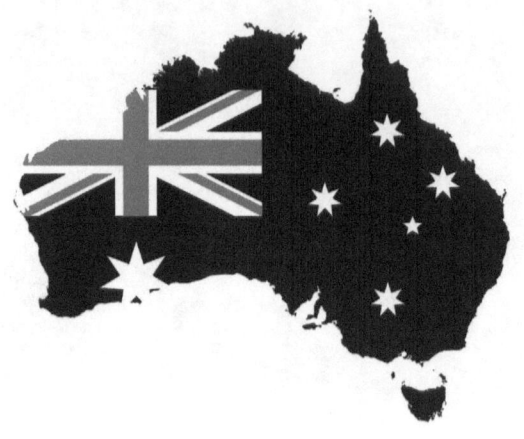

164. CUBA

Coca-Cola isn't sold in Cuba.

165. ICE

Hot water freezes faster than cold water.

166. HARP

A harp has 47 strings.

167. RGB

Every color is made up of red, green, and blue.

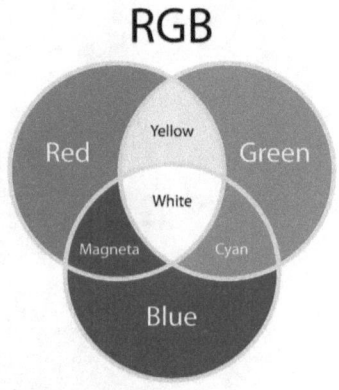

168. VIOLIN

Playing the violin burns approximately 170 calories per hour.

169. OVERMORROW

The English word for "the day after tomorrow" is "overmorrow."

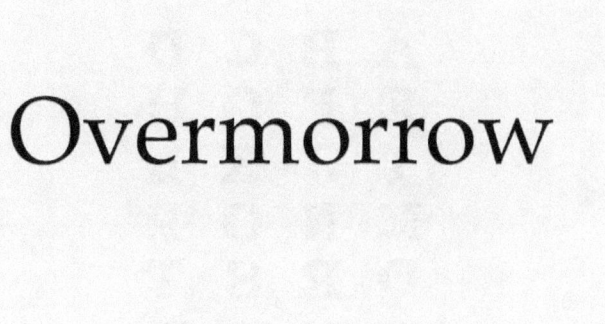

170. SMALLEST GUITAR

The world's smallest guitar is 10 micrometers long.

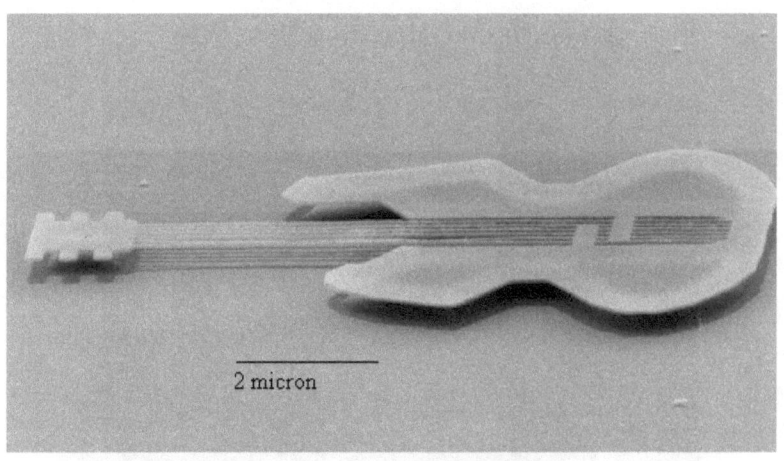

171. ALPHABET

The word "alphabet" comes from the first two letters of the Greek alphabet: alpha, bēta.

```
A  B  C  D
E  F  G  H
I  J  K  L
M  N  O  P
Q  R  S  T
U  V  W  X
   Y  Z
```

172. THE HIMALAYAS

The Himalayas were formed 50 million years ago.

173. YAHOO

"Yahoo" is an acronym for "Yet Another Hierarchical Officious Oracle!"

174. PIN

PIN is an acronym for Personal Identification Number.

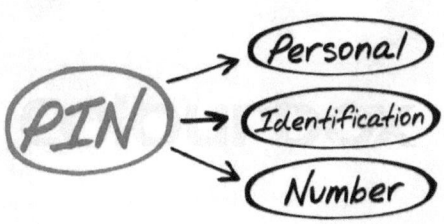

175. AVATAR

The highest grossing movie of all time is Avatar.

176. SNICKERS

Snickers is the best selling candy bar in the world.

177. NAURU

Nauru is the only country in the world without an official capital.

178. METRIC SYSTEM

The metric system was invented in France.

179. BIGGEST GUITAR

The world's biggest functioning guitar is 13 meters long.

180. BIG BEN

Big Ben chimed for the first time on July 11th 1859.

181. VINCENT VAN GOGH

The artist Vincent Van Gogh cut off his left ear.

182. DUBAI MALL

The world's biggest shopping mall is Dubai Mall.

183. PEARS

There are over 3000 varieties of pears.

184. BASKETBALL

An inventor named James Naismith invented basketball.

185. ONE EYE OPEN

Dolphins sleep with one eye open.

186. GREECE

80% of Greece is made up of mountains.

187. PLASTIC BOTTLE

Plastic bottles take around 450 years to break down!

188. CAR

An average car has over 30,000 parts.

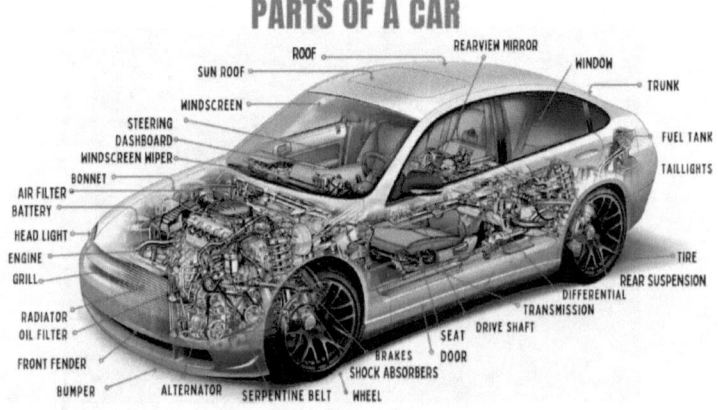

189. FIRST COMPUTER

The world's first computer weighed more than 27 tons.

190. POMOLOGY

The study of fruits is known as pomology.

191. TALC

Talc is the softest mineral in the World.

192. BARREL

There are 159 litres of oil in a barrel.

193. LEGO PRODUCTION

The LEGO factory produces around 36,000 pieces of lego every minute.

194. SKULK

A group of foxes is called a skulk.

195. DANNEBROG

The flag of Denmark is called the "Dannebrog" which translates to "Danish cloth."

196. CHROMOPHOBIA

Chromophobia is the fear of colours.

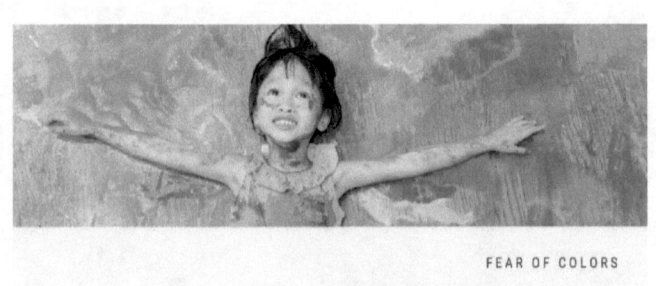

197. FORESTS

Forests cover 31% of the Earth's surface area.

198. -200 DEG CELSIUS

The average surface temperature on Neptune is about -200 degrees Celsius.

199. HELICOPTER

The longest distance traveled in a helicopter without landing is 3,562 kilometres.

200. MOST VISITED COUNTRY

France is the most visited country in the world.

201. GARAGE START UPS

Amazon, Apple, and Google all started in garages.

202. EARTHS CIRCUMFERENCE

The Earth's circumference is 40,075 kilometres.

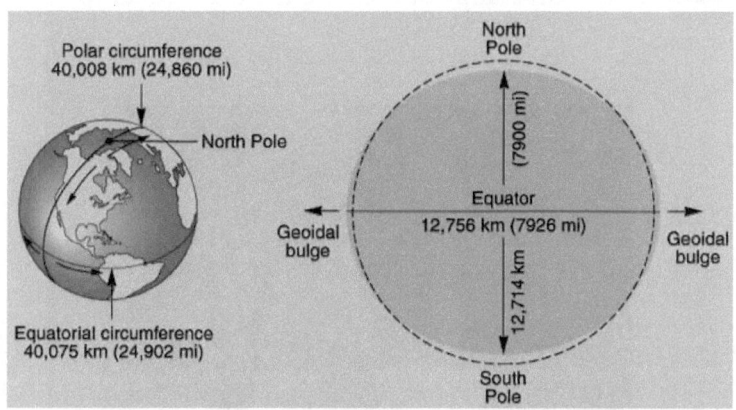

203. BLACKLETTER

Blackletter, also known as Old English, Gothic, or Fraktur was the first ever font.

204. DASH

A "dash" is actually a unit of measurement. It's equal to 1/8 of a teaspoon.

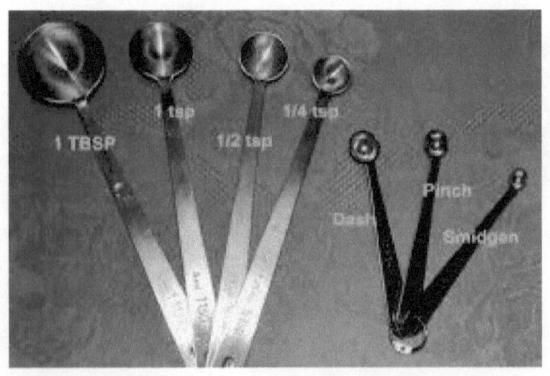

205. HORSES

Horses can't breathe through their mouths.

206. BAND-AID

The Band-Aid was invented in 1920 by Earle Dickson.

207. WALT DISNEY

Walt Disney Pictures was founded on October 16th 1923.

208. SPEED OF LIGHT

The speed of light is 299,792,458 metres per second.

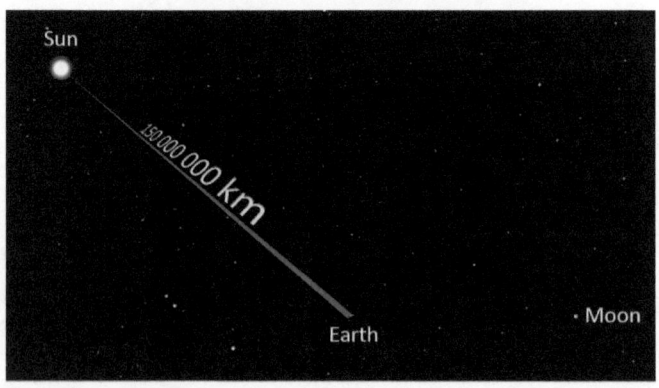

209. PARKER 51

The Parker 51 is the world's most sold fountain pen of all time.

210. NOKIA 1100

The best-selling phone of all time is the Nokia 1100.

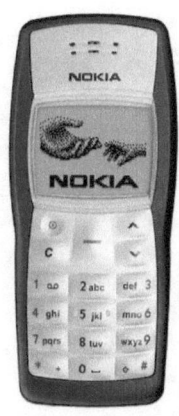

211. FIRE

Earth is the only planet in our solar system where fire can burn.

212. GROCERY SHOPPING

The average time spent grocery shopping (per trip) is 46 minutes.

213. MOUSE

The computer mouse was invented by NASA.

214. MELTING POINT

The melting point of diamond is 4,027 degrees Celsius.

215. CORN

Corn is grown on every continent except Antarctica.

216. ADIDAS & PUMA

The founders of Adidas and Puma are brothers.

217. CHECKMATE

The word "Checkmate" in chess comes from the Persian phrase "Shāh Māt (شاه مات)" meaning "the king is helpless"!

218. SECONDS IN A WEEK

There are 604,800 seconds in a week.

> ### Example 1
>
> - How many seconds are in a week?
>
> - How many seconds in a minute? 60 seconds
> - How many minutes in an hour? 60 minutes
> - How many hours in a day? 24 hours
> - How many days in a week? 7 days
>
> 60 x 60 x 24 x 7 = 604,800 seconds

219. THE STATUE OF LIBERTY

The Statue of Liberty took 30 years to oxidize. The Statue of Liberty is made of copper, and after some time, copper changes from its dull-brown colour to a bright green colour due to oxidation.

220. ACCIDENT

The first ever car accident occurred in 1891.

221. AUGUST

More people celebrate their birthdays in August than in any other month.

222. B FOR BILLION

If you wrote out every number (one, two, three, etc.) you wouldn't use the letter "b" before one billion.

223. SUN

The Sun is 4.603 billion years old.

224. WEIGHT ON MARS

Your weight on Mars is 37.83% of your weight on Earth.

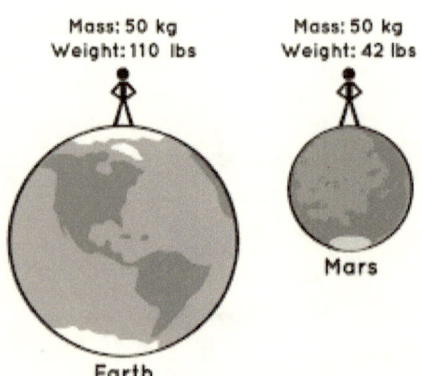

225. ALPHABET "J"

The last letter added to the English alphabet was "J"! It used to be a fancier way of writing the letter "I".

226. ABSTEMIOUS

The word "abstemious" has all of the vowels in order.

Abstemious

227. ANTARCTICA

Antarctica is technically a desert.

228. PORSCHE

Porsche's first car was electric. It was powered by an "octagonal electric motor."

229. JAM OR MARMALADE

The difference between jam and marmalade is the way they are made; marmalade is made with citrus.

230. 111111111

111111111 multiplied by itself is equal to 12345678987654321!

```
           1×1 = 1
          11×11 = 121
         111×111 = 12321
        1111×1111 = 1234321
       11111×11111 = 123454321
      111111×111111 = 12345654321
     1111111×1111111 = 1234567654321
    11111111×11111111 = 123456787654321
   111111111×111111111 = 12345678987654321
```

231. MATH

Humans have been doing Math since around 30,000 BC.

232. TOMATOES

There are around 10,000 varieties of tomatoes worldwide.

233. HEADPHONES

In 1910, an engineer named Nathaniel Baldwin invented headphones.

234. JIFFY

A 'jiffy' is an actual unit of time. It means 1/100th of a second.

235. MELTING POINT OF GOLD

The melting point of gold is 1,064 degrees Celsius.

236. DOGS

'Dogs can only see blue, yellow and some shades of grey. If you were to throw a red ball into a green field, it'd be very difficult for them to see it.

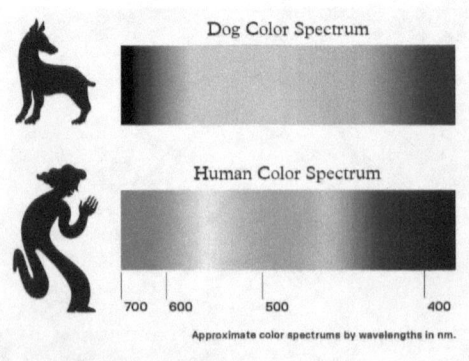

237. FIRST WEB PAGE

The world's first web page went up on the 6th of August 1991.

World Wide Web

The WorldWideWeb (W3) is a wide-area hypermedia information retrieval initiative aiming to give universal access to a large universe of documents.

Everything there is online about W3 is linked directly or indirectly to this document, including an executive summary of the project, Mailing lists , Policy , November's W3 news , Frequently Asked Questions .

What's out there?
    Pointers to the world's online information, subjects , W3 servers, etc.
Help
    on the browser you are using
Software Products
    A list of W3 project components and their current state. (e.g. Line Mode ,X11 Viola , NeXTStep , Servers , Tools , Mail robot , Library)
Technical
    Details of protocols, formats, program internals etc
Bibliography
    Paper documentation on W3 and references.
People
    A list of some people involved in the project.
History
    A summary of the history of the project.
How can I help ?
    If you would like to support the web..
Getting code
    Getting the code by anonymous FTP , etc.

238. TRAIN

The word "train" is derived from the Latin *trahere* meaning "to pull" or "to draw"!

239. 3 DOGS

Three dogs survived the Titanic sinking.

240. STRAWBERRIES

Strawberries are the only fruits with seeds on the outside.

241. 80 KMPH

Lions can run a maximum of 80 kilometres per hour.

242. COTTON CANDY

Cotton candy was invented by a dentist!

243. COALITION

A group of cheetahs is called a coalition.

244. DREAMT

"Dreamt" is the only English word that ends in the letters "mt."

Dreamt

245. MARS – GOD OF WAR

Mars is named after the roman god of war.

246. JUPITER

Jupiter is 300 times larger than the Earth.

247. POTATO

Potatoes are 80% water!

248. FLUTE

The flute was invented in 900 BCE.

249. MICROWAVE

The microwave was invented in 1946.

250. SQUARE FLAG

Switzerland and the Vatican City are the only two countries with square-shaped flags.

251. DISNEY WORLD

Disney World first opened in 1971!

252. VOLCANOES

Indonesia has the most volcanoes of any country in the world.

253. ZERO

There is no roman numeral for zero.

254. FOUR

"Four" is the only number that is spelt with the same number of letters as the number itself.

255. FORTY

"Forty" is the only number that is spelled with letters in alphabetical order.

256. SEVEN

Opposite sides on a dice always add up to seven.

257. LEMNISCATE

The name of the infinity symbol is "lemniscate."

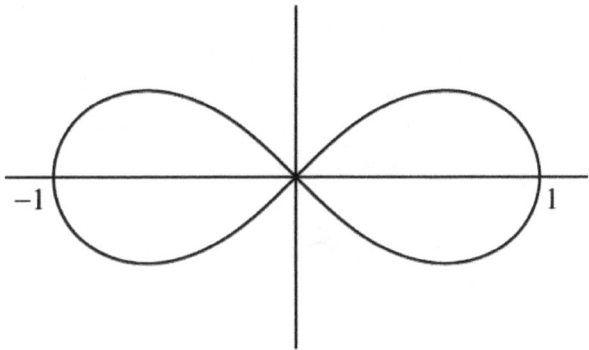

258. RHYTHM

"Rhythm" is the longest English word without vowels.

259. FOLDING CHAIR

Folding Chairs were invented in 1947.

260. SPRINKLER

The sprinkler was invented in 1871.

261. BIRDS

Birds don't have teeth.

262. WINDMILL

The windmill was invented in 1854.

263. TOWER

A group of giraffes is called a tower.

264. AIR CONDITIONERS

Air Conditioners were invented in 1902.

265. GRAVITY

Jupiter has the most gravity in our solar system.

266. CUCKOO CLOCK

The cuckoo clock was invented in 1629.

267. CORNFLAKES

Cornflakes were invented in 1894.

268. EMAIL

Email was invented in 1978.

269. SMALLEST BONE

The smallest bone in your body is in your ear.

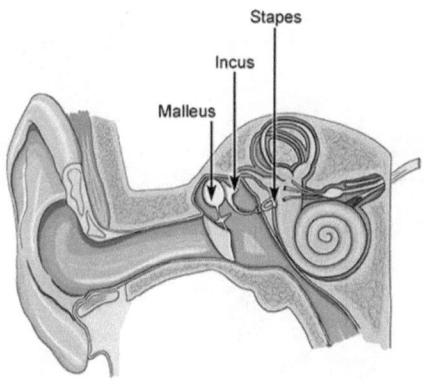

270. THE MOON

The Moon's phases repeat every 29.5 days, but it's orbit around the Earth only takes 27 days.

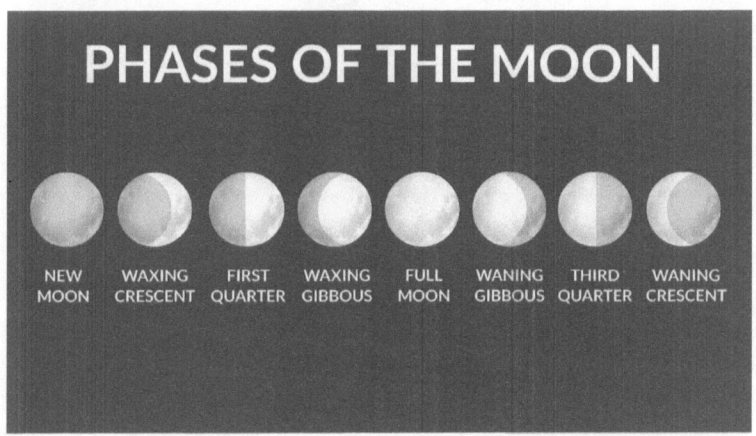

271. 2 STOMACHS

Dolphins have two stomachs.

272. THE DOORBELL

The doorbell was invented in 1831.

273. MONA LISA

The Mona Lisa doesn't have eyebrows.

274. GOOGLE

The most visited website ever is https://www.google.com.

275. BALE

A group of turtles is called a bale.

276. ELEPHANTS

Elephant's can't jump.

277. 1 YEAR

One year doesn't have 365 days, it actually has 365.2422 days.

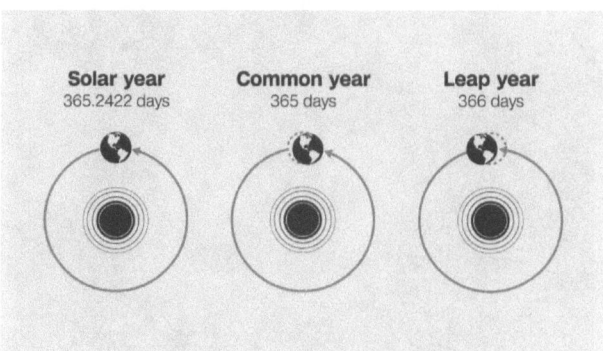

278. MOONLIGHT

The Moon does not make its own light; "Moonlight" is actually reflected sunlight.

279. ORANGE

The colour orange was named after the fruit, and not vice versa.

280. NOT BERRIES

Blackberries and raspberries aren't berries.

281. BERRIES

Bananas, pumpkins, avocados and cucumbers are berries.

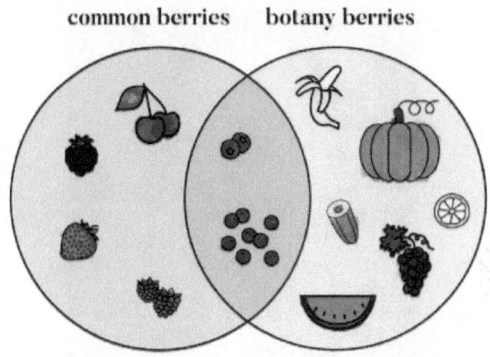

282. PARLIAMENT

A group of owls is called a parliament.

283. 1700 WORDS

William Shakespeare is credited with the invention or introduction of over 1,700 words that are still used in English today.

284. PRINGLES CHIP

The shape of a Pringles chip is called a hyperbolic paraboloid.

285. CAPTCHA

CAPTCHA is an acronym for "Completely Automated Public Turing Test to tell Computers and Humans Apart!"

286. THE JAZZ SINGER

The first film with sound was made in 1927 and was called "The Jazz Singer."

287. SHIVER

A group of sharks is called a "shiver"

288. FLAMBOYANCE

A flock of flamingos is called a "flamboyance."

289. NORDIC CROSS

All Scandinavian countries have a cross in their flags.

290. LEFT-HANDED

Just 10% of all the people in the world are left-handed

291. TASTE BUDS

You lose around 30% of your taste buds while on a plane.

292. DIAMOND RAIN

It rains diamonds on Saturn.

293. LETHOLOGICA

The term for when you can't remember a word is "lethologica."

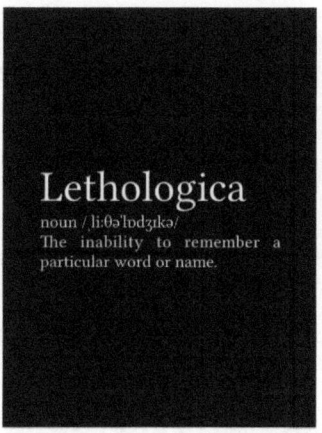

294. AIBOHPHOBIA

The phobia of palindromes (words that are the same forwards and backwards) is called aibohphobia.

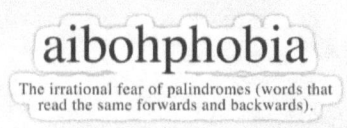

295. BABY FLAMINGOS

Baby flamingos are born grey not pink.

296. TURN ORANGE

If you eat too many carrots, your skin will actually turn slightly orange.

297. MUSCLES

There are more than 600 muscles in the human body.

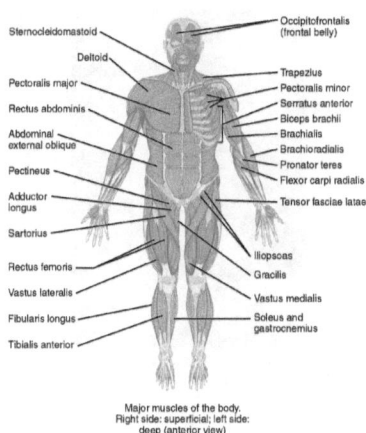

Major muscles of the body.
Right side: superficial; left side: deep (anterior view)

298. LOL

The acronym "LOL" was added to the Oxford English Dictionary in 2011.

299. ARMY

A group of frogs is called an army.

300. 3 HEARTS

Octopuses have three hearts.

Two of the hearts work exclusively to move blood past the animal's gills, where it releases carbon dioxide and gains oxygen. Then, the third heart circulates that oxygen-rich blood to the organs and muscles, giving them energy.

301. #LOVE

#love is the most used hashtag on Instagram.

302. FIRST TELEVISION ADVERTISEMENT

The world's first television advertisement was for a company named Bulova Watches and aired on July 1st, 1941.

303. THE LAST SUPPER

The Last Supper took Leonardo Da Vinci three years to paint.

304. NETHERLANDS

The Netherlands is the largest exporter of flowers in the world.

305. ABU DHABI

Abu Dhabi, the capital of the UAE, is the largest emirate and accounts for about 87% of the UAE's total area.

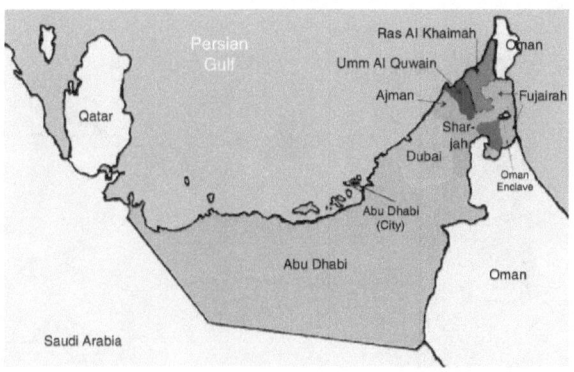

306. TAYLOR SWIFT

Taylor Swift's "All Too Well (10 Minute Version)" is the longest song to ever reach the number one spot in the Billboard Hot 100.

307. HONEY

Pure honey has almost zero moisture due to which bacteria cannot grow or survive in it. This is probably the sole reason why honey does not get spoiled for a long time.

308. BALLPOINT PEN

The average writing length of a ballpoint pen is 900 metres.

309. FINGERPRINTS

Identical twins don't have the same fingerprints.

310. CLOUD

The average cloud weighs around 500,000 kilograms.

311. DAYLIGHT SAVING

72 countries currently use Daylight Saving Time.

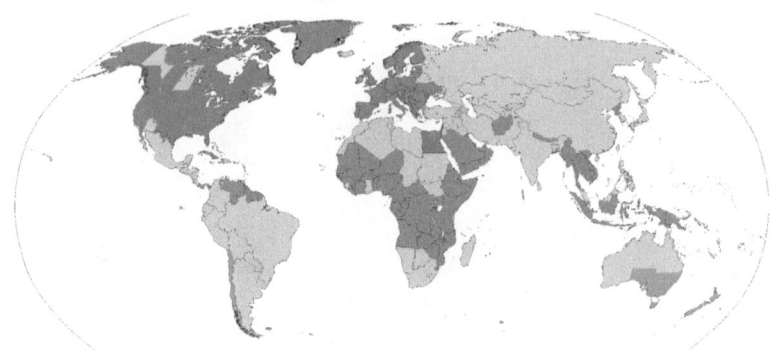

312. NEPAL

Nepal has more public holidays than any other country: 35

313. EARTH'S ROTATION

The Earth's rotation is gradually slowing. This means that, on average, the length of a day increases by around 1.8 seconds per century. 600 million years ago a day lasted just 21 hours.

314. SHEEP V/S HUMAN

New Zealand has more sheep than humans.

315. BRAIN BURNS CALORIES

Your brain burns 400-500 calories a day.

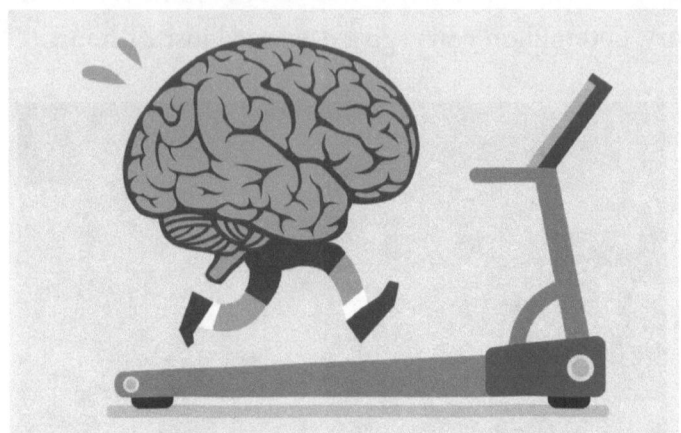

316. SKIN

The skin is the largest organ of the body.

317. NORTHERN HEMISPHERE

Approximately 90% of the Earth's population lives in the northern hemisphere.

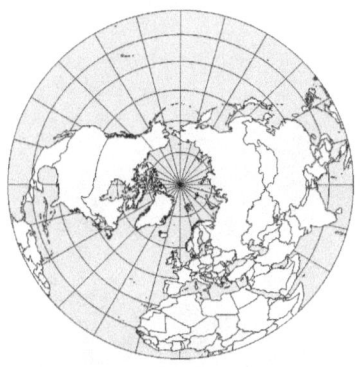

318. AUSTRALIA- WIDER THAN THE MOON

Australia is wider than the moon. According to NASA, the moon's equatorial diameter is 3,476 km, whereas Australia's width from east to west is almost 4,000 km.

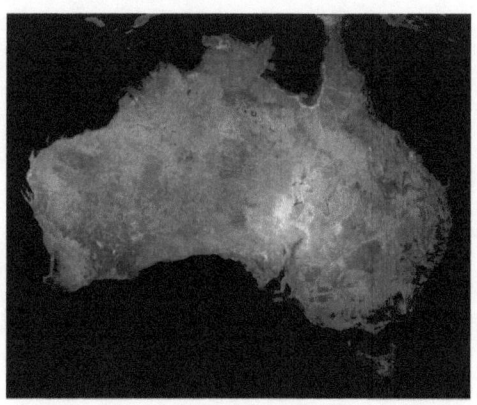

319. EIFFEL TOWER

The Eiffel Tower was originally made for Barcelona. Gustave Eiffel originally submitted his design to Barcelona, but the city turned it down.

320. PYRAMIDS - SUDAN

Sudan has more pyramids than any country in the world.

321. FINLAND

Finland has been named the world's happiest country for the seventh year in a row.

322. HEARTBEATS

Your heart beats an average of 100,000 times each day.

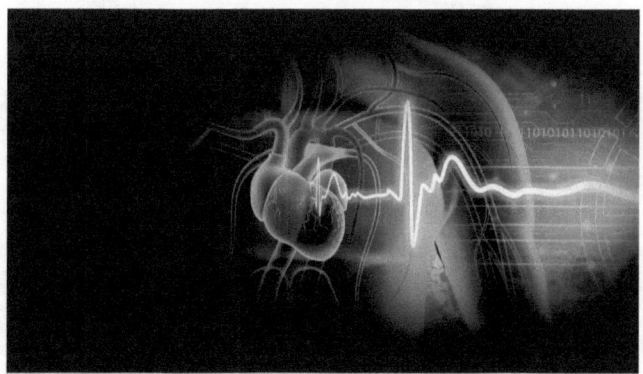

323. RUSSIA

Russia has 11 time zones.

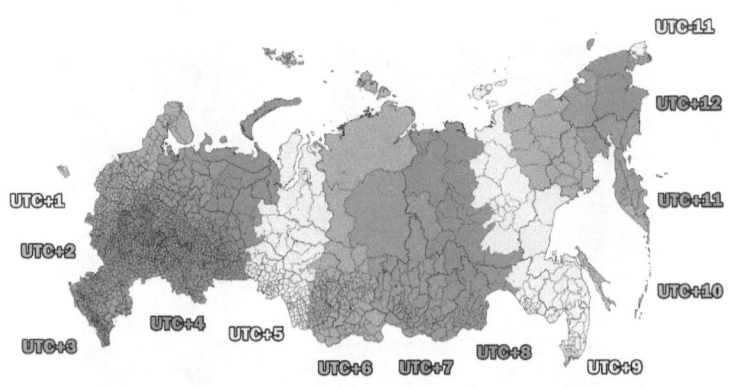

324. TUG OF WAR

Tug-of-war used to be an Olympic sport.

325. LONGEST CAR

The Cadillac limousine, the world's longest car, is 30.48 metres long and has 26 tires.

326. CENTRE OF THE EARTH

The Burj Khalifa's elevator moves at It would take just 19 minutes to fall to the centre of the earth.

327. LARGEST CASTLE

The largest castle in the world, Malbork Castle, is in Poland.

328. GUINNESS BOOK

The first ever Guinness Book of World Records was published on 27th August 1955.

329. MONTREAL TOWER

Montreal Tower is 165 metres tall and is inclined at angle of 45°, making it the tallest inclined building in the world.

330. USA'S CAPITAL

The USA's capital has changed nine times!

331. TEETH

Human teeth are the only part of the body that can't heal themselves.

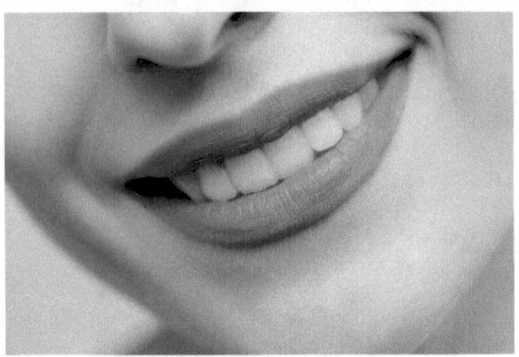

332. SHORTEST WAR

The Anglo-Zanzibar War was a military conflict fought between the United Kingdom and the Sultanate of Zanzibar on 27 August 1896. The conflict lasted between 38 and 45 minutes, marking it as the shortest recorded war in history.

333. SEA WORLD – ABU DHABI

SeaWorld, Abu Dhabi's aquarium contains approximately 25 million litres of water, making it the largest aquarium in the world.

334. OSTRICH'S EYE

An ostrich's eye is bigger than its brain.

335. SNEEZE

A sneeze travels out of your mouth at over 100 miles per hour.

336. HASHTAG

The hashtag symbol is actually called "octothorp."

337. AFRICA

Africa is the only continent in all four hemispheres.

338. TONGUE PRINT

Like fingerprints, everyone's tongue print is unique.

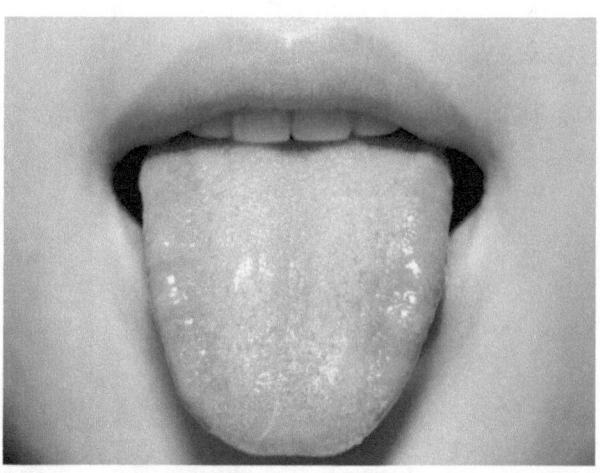

339. HOLLYWOOD

The Hollywood sign used to say Hollywoodland.

340. EIFFEL TOWER DURING THE SUMMER

The Eiffel Tower can be 15 cm taller during the summer, due to thermal expansion.

341. HUM

You can't hum while you're pinching your nose.

342. SPEEDING TICKET

The first speeding ticket was issued in 1896. It was given to a Mr Walter Arnold in Kent, UK. Mr Arnold was driving an early car at 8 miles per hour in a zone where the speed limit was 2 mph.

343. VENUS

Venus is the hottest planet in our solar system.

344. HEART

The heart is the only muscle that never gets tired.

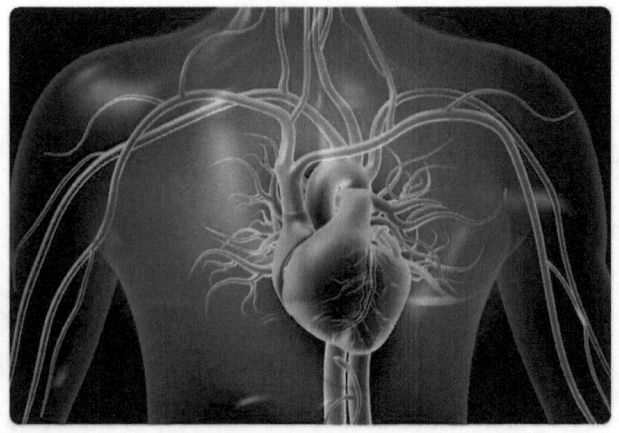

345. LUNGS

Your left lung is smaller than your right lung, to create room for your heart,

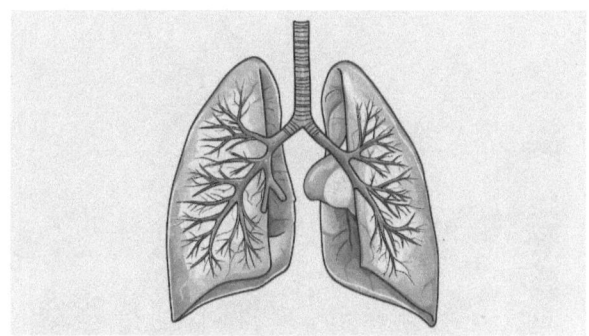

346. DIAMONDS

Diamonds were mined for the first time in India.

347. PINEAPPLE

Pineapple plants produce only one fruit, and it could take 2-3 years to develop edible fruit, sometimes even longer.

348. KITKAT

Japan has over 300 Kit Kat flavours, including melon, wasabi, baked potato and vegetable juice.

349. PIGS

Pigs cannot look up at the sky. It's due to the anatomy of their neck muscles and spine.

350. NAILS

Our nails grow faster in summer due to increased blood supply to the fingertips.

351. KETCHUP

In the 1830s, tomato ketchup was sold as a medicine.

352. BAMBOO

Contrary to popular belief, bamboo is classified as a type of grass not a type of tree.

353. HIPPOPOTAMUS

Hippopotamuses can't swim.

354. COWS HAVE ACCENTS

Cows have different accents. They will moo differently deoending on which region of the world they come from.

355. CARROTS

Carrots were orignally purple.

356. SPAGHETTO

A single strand of spaghetti is called a "spaghetto."

357. PENCIL

An average pencil has enough graphite to draw a line 56 kilometres long.

358. LEWIS HAMILTON

Lewis Hamilton has won 105 Formula One Grand Prix races to date, more than any other Formula One driver.

359. NOVAK DJOKOVIC

Tennis player Novak Djokovic has won 24 Grand Slam titles, more than any other player.

360. SPENCER GORE

An English sportsman named Spencer Gore won the first ever Wimbledon Championship in the year 1877.

361. CHESS GRANDMASTER

Abhimanyu Mishra became a chess grandmaster at the age of 12 years old, making him the youngest person to ever do so.

362. OLDEST NBA TEAM

The Sacramento Kings formed in 1923, making them the oldest team in the NBA.

363. LARGEST HOTEL

Malaysia's First World Hotel has 7,351 rooms, making it the largest hotel in the world.

364. BILL RUSSELL

NBA player Bill Russell has won 11 championships, making him the most successful NBA player of all time.

365. GOODBYE

The practice of saying goodbye goes back centuries, with first evidence of the interjection found around 1565–75. It's a contraction of the phrase "God be with ye."

www.ingramcontent.com/pod-product-compliance
Lightning Source LLC
LaVergne TN
LVHW041710070526
838199LV00045B/1279